Sue Ann Martinson

CHANGING WOMAN

with drawings by

Susan Lee/Susanah Libana

Some of these poems have appeared in the following publications:
**Aspen Writer's Conference Anthology, Great River Review, Milkweed
Chronicle, Sackbut Review,** and **Yet Another Small Magazine,** and in
the anthology, **Border Crossings** (New Rivers Press).

ISBN: 0-911051-27-9
Library of Congress Number:
85 - 062188

PLAIN VIEW PRESS
1509 Dexter
Austin, Texas 78704

Member COSMEP

CONTENTS

III

ABOUT THE ARTIST

*Susan Lee (Susanah Libana) is a graduate of the University of Texas, Vanderbilt and L'Academie Royale des Beaux Arts of Brussels, Belgium, where she received a diploma in sculpture in 1967. Since then she has worked with sculpture, jewelry, poetry, songs, video-tapes and slidetapes. The slidetape, **From Spiral to Spear,** a study of ancient female and male roles, symbols and legends, led to her discovery of goddesses and returning to sculpture as her primary work. The goddesses represent a system of values in which harmony with ever-changing nature and other beings is primary, and in which women's abilities and creativity have been honored throughout the world since paleolithic times and into the present.*

The goddesses are miniature (mostly wearable) sculptures, produced by the lost-wax method in brass, bronze, sterling silver and gold. The designs are sometimes inspired by artifacts from throughout the world, sometimes derived from Susan's imagination. They represent distinct qualities, talents and values and can be used as symbolic magic to focus thought and behavior in order to achieve goals and deal positively with change.

The drawings in this book are based on the Navajo goddess, Changing Woman, and Susan's research of Native American goddesses.

*To order jewelry, Susan Lee may be contacted at **Ssymbols,** 218 Dickson, Fayetteville, AR 72701, (501) 521 - 5132. Send a business-size, self-addressed, stamped envelope for a catalog of 40 designs in the form of pendants, earrings, rings, buckles and altar pieces, and for information about renting the slidetape **From Spiral to Spear.***

Sue Ann Martinson was born and raised in Minnesota. She is the only daughter of five children born to a mother from Kansas whose ancestors came over on the Mayflower and fought in the Revolutionary and Civil Wars, and a father whose storekeeper father came to South Dakota from Norway at the turn of the century, and whose mother's Norwegian parents came to Wisconsin a generation earlier. Music was the center of activity in her home as she was growing up, her father being a church choir director, her mother a church organist. From her parents she learned a love of music, and of land and heritage.

Ms. Martinson attended Lawrence University in Appleton, Wisconsin, and received a Master's Degree in English from the University of Minnesota. Active in the Twin Cities literary community, she was the first coordinator of The Loft, A Place for Writing and Literature, and of the Great Midwestern Bookshow, a small press book fair. She is founding and current editor of Sing Heavenly Muse! *, a journal of women's poetry and prose.*

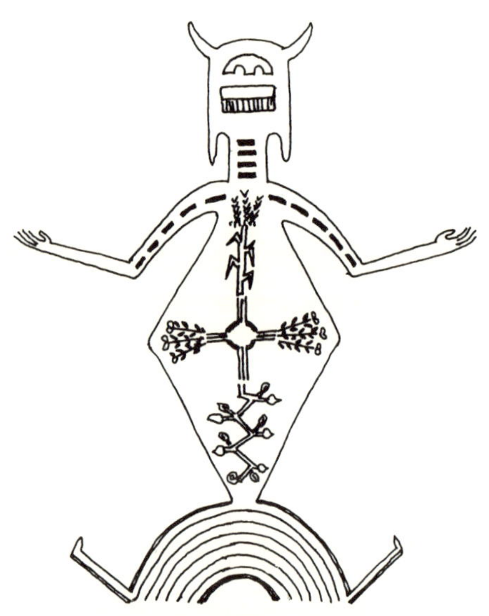

I

Changing Woman, harmony of
wind lightning storm animal
divine in all we hear
see feel touch

NAVAJO RAINBOW GODDESS: PROTECTION

PRAIRIE

This vague uneasiness—
born of the longing of children of children
who covered sunlit stretches
of prairie day after day, never stopping
never losing the moment of beauty

We reached destinations:
now we move intensely
across the land by bus, car, plane
forgetting it was this we came for

I came with my ancestors across the Atlantic,
Mayflower masts into the wind.
I saw the light in the steeple —
one if by land, two if by sea.
From Virginia, to Illinois, to Kansas
I moved across vast stretches of bold prairie
in wagon trains, my bonnet hanging at the back
of my neck when I could not bear its primness
on my head. I lifted my skirts through prairie
grasses, saw the unmistakable arch of rat feet
scurrying into the brush. I have birthed in a wagon,
the baby sending her tremulous notes out
over the prairie to mix with cricket and bird. At night
I huddled to the whisper of crickets, the croak
of tree frogs. I listened to rain sing
on the wagon top far into the night. When I woke
the prairie sang, pink spires laced with sun, yellow,
lavender, and white under an intense blue sky.

Concrete and flat land, flat buildings
with signs painted colors that do not capture
the gaiety of that lost prairie.
Concrete with no green, buildings rising
willy nilly out of the earth. Air of chemicals
and smoke, where I cannot see or breathe.

I draw murals and flowers of bright colors
on concrete, try to re-create the prairie
in neon, fluorescents that glow in the dark
against the cold stone of city buildings

*my roots are rootlessness
movement, light, intensity, color*

I want vast stretches of prairie
to lie before me, I want to travel forever
on days and nights like this

I have danced on this prairie before,
seen the sun rise and set. I have bowed
to the flowers and they to me, slept
in the open under stars and moon, under
a tree in the rain. I have stood
in the green/yellow, blue/yellow intensity
of an August afternoon, the prairie stretching
out before me like an omen:

*It was for this I came
For this I travelled across oceans,
through wars, for this I died
The journey has barely begun*

CIRCLE OF STONE

my mother was old
her house burned
ash blew on the wind
scattered to four
                corners of the earth
now every heart is a stone
each flower's bloom
each tree's fruit
brightly colored stone

the mother is
            a core of fire
the mother is
            a wind stone
the mother is
            a life stone
the mother is
            a circle of stone

out of the ashes
out of the ashes
every heart
            a brightly colored stone

BLACK GOLD

Trying to wake up
suddenly I am sleepy
I have no coffee this morning

      That black liquid I was taught to consume
      in quantities by Norwegian grandmothers
      to save myself from the frigid north
      There must be something of the green and humus
      of the jungle in that liquid
      sun and heat and gold
      black gold

      And the Kaffee Klatches in blue and white Norwegian kitchens
      sun pouring in the window on a cold winter day
      sandbakkels and pastries rich with filling and white frosting

      my Norwegian father, gone now
      his brothers and my Aunt Ann gone, too
      I remember them all singing
      raising their throaty voices into the earth

      my father, his tenor voice clear and full
      like lilies deep-rooted in the ground
      When he sang people trembled.
      moved into realms beyond

I close my eyes
lips come from nowhere
brush my cheek
angels

I'll not be able to work
until I have a cup of coffee

TEXTURES

the texture of waves on a clear day
they move slowly on water
create and re-create

texture always surprises me
like this jacket I am wearing
turquoise, black, teal blue, and wine
tightly woven chenille
yet so different from the smooth hand

the hand   the palm smooth   lines
the birth line   the life line
the hand is not really smooth
fine lines that cross and criss-cross
pores   your body breathes through

the texture of breath
on a cold day   steam
each of us breathes   sends out
small waves   into the world

YOU TRY TO LEAVE ME TO NATURE

You grew like a stump
short and squat
until I could no longer
hold you in

one day I looked
    and you had tall loping stems
    branching loosely in the air
    their arch sweeping, bending
    with a new-found presence
    wind rustling through a shimmering green so rich
    the eyes of spring cannot equal that sungold ripeness

We curl and cling
two trees unfurling
trunks grow together
sucking earth's sweetness
drawing the new rain
    through each branch
    each leaf
    every vein and leafy point saluting

You sleep beside me now
my head on the curve of your shoulder
or your head at my breast

our tongues curl and touch
linger
brush lips, hair
caress crevices

our bark roughens with age
protects the greenness of our core

we lap the wind

the little ball says to the big ball
  no
  now if we hit this bowl, here
  then we'll be at the right angle
  for that bowl, there

  soft tone
  now hard
  loud
  oops— not that angle
  thud

  oh— a good clear tone
  high and sweet
  then quick
  two hits

  now swing me wide
  inside that medium bowl
  a deep rich sound

  dance me now
  for the kids
  big and little

nine vermillion bowls
an iron black ball
a small white ball of wood
strung at opposite ends of a pole
the pole hanging by a string
the string attached at the end of the heavy ball

slow, slow . . .
now quick
ricochet
spin round

the challenge is to get me inside the big bowl
where I've never been known to land

THANKSGIVING MORNING

1

I drive across a quiet city
leafless trees, frosty ground
foreshadow winter

I think of the colors of death:
the yellow of old age
the blue of cancer
the red of violence
the black of the death camps

2

"A nineteen-year-old detainee, Mr. Mtimkulu, was held
in connection with a demonstration against the government.
Upon his release he took seriously ill and doctors found
that he had been poisoned with a rare insecticide used
overseas. The South African police are refusing to comment."

And in El Salvador, El Salvador, the bodies grow
on trees, fed by the blood-soaked earth. The priest says,
We will all die. He is killed a week later
while saying mass in a hospital.

More money for missiles. Unemployment rises.
Ethiopian children stare curiously with rich brown eyes
as a TV cameraman captures their swollen bellies.

The Polish prisons swell with workers, the food lines
grow longer. What is it, not to be able to say
what you think, to have to whisper across tables
in crowded restaurants, in corners,
that you can do nothing
because they have the guns and tanks.

3

I remember
the photographic shadow
of a Japanese
on the side of a stone building
This was a person
Hiroshima Mon Amour

Mon Amour
Mon Amour

You can't break
this heart of stone

AFTER TEN YEARS

Neodesha at twilight,
another small town
on the Kansas plain
Main Street, two blocks long
my uncle's law office
in an old brick building
at the center of town

a phosphorescent light
filters through low-cast clouds
this muggy day —
the locusts' incessant whir
small town restlessness in earthy quiet

in Minnesota this air
would mean a tornado —
these yellow streaks bold as sun
belong only to Kansas towns at twilight

in this house
I spent long summer afternoons
in the world of cousins
my aunt presiding over
onion, cucumber and tomato,
iced tea, and fresh sweet corn
from their farm just outside of town

here, I learned the talk of farmers—
weather, crops— what it is to watch
day by day
corn pierce the sun

I lean on the cool red brick
trace the screened porches
where we slept those hot summer nights
awakening to see the beds of prize-winning iris

on the concrete slabs of the front porch
I made snakes under a Forth of July sun
while my brothers
lit firecrackers under tin cans

the yellow sky I do not remember
matches roses on the pale wallpaper,
the piano is still by the window
and the locusts' song
does not fade

THE OMEN

two sparrows flit
in and out of tree branches

a red balloon
held tightly
by a budding tree
hangs over the street
bouncing in the wind

as I leave the grocery
store, a crow caws
clearly, twice

I think — not yet—
not yet will you have me
my eyes to peck out
flesh to dust

Cawwww   Cawww
suddenly her/our purpose is clear
she, the crow, is with us
no nuclear holocaust
no war   no slaughter
no black death
beyond imagination
no white death
beyond imagination

Cawwwww   Cawwww

on the edge of consciousness
glistening black against blue sky
her wings spread with purpose

somewhere close by
now   a robin sings
guards the day

CHIAROSCURO

Snow-light
      at the edge of darkness
my cold apple core
falls into cold snow

ivory white
      on pure white
resting on my cheek
resting on my tongue
making patterns
on my mittens and coat
falls
    to melt silently
    or disappear into the bank of snow

in spring
      small brown seeds
may sink beneath intricate snowflakes
linked
    across the dark edge of earth
    this fall of light

II

From lightning, straight and true,
you gave us tongue
from skywater, tears

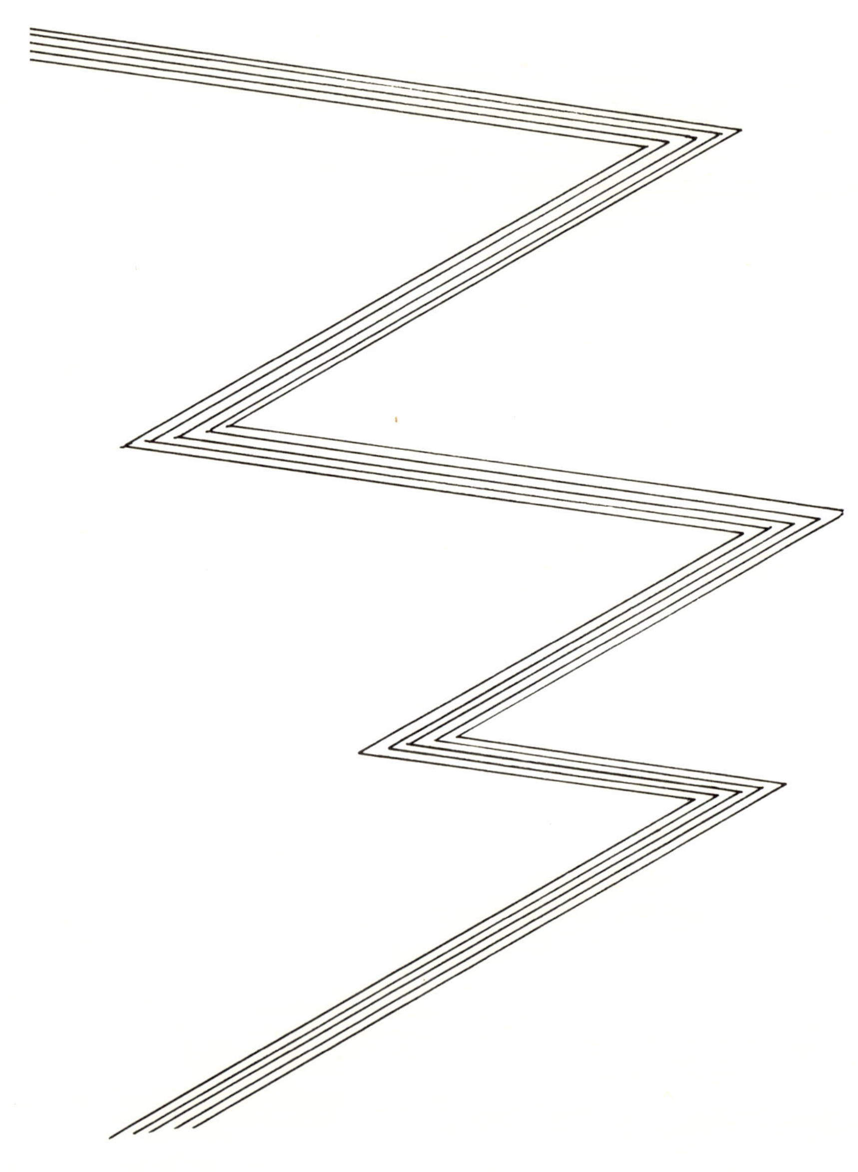

CHANGING WOMAN(MOON)
Navajo Legend

In the western waters you dwell
teacher of the Blessing Way
your mother, the darkness
your father, the dawn.
We hear you on the wind.

You wove our hair of darkness
our skull of dawn
our flesh of red-white stone.

You made our toe and finger nails of cool abalone
our bone and brains, our white of eye, of white shell,
our pupils of slivered mica and rock crystal
our ear lobes of red-white stone.

You gave us beads of shell for hearing,
teeth of shell, nose of abalone.
From plants of all kinds
you wove our pubic hair, our pores,
from a rainbow, our arms.
From lightning straight and true, you gave us tongue,
from skywater, tears.

Changing Woman, harmony of
wind lightning storm animal
divine in all we hear
    see feel touch

pouring the sky
        out of your gold cup

half-moon oracle
            0-gape
        eyes blinded to earth

bowl
    catch me
            let me fall inside
            your golden circle

until your eyes
            glow again
on this small earth space

FACES

A little ballerina with blond hair
steps forth every noon
from a clock's small wood door
pirouettes on slender legs
to the sound of tinkling chimes,
her white dress sparkling.

The moon face of the village half-wit
stares at the tower clock
as the hands, medieval curved arrowheads,
point the time of day.

He steps to the clockmaker's window
waits
as every day he waits
for the pageant to unfold.

The tower clock tolls twelve
ringing   ringing   ringing

and the moon face smiles

This gallery has unicorns everywhere, carved wooden unicorns lying on logs, pewter and gold mosaic unicorns in bright buckles, unicorn corkscrews, and unicorn cards. And the unicorn sculpture outside the gallery—pink-beige, rearing and prancing, its ass like a young girl's, sleek and unhaired. Give me the real thing, a unicorn to tame, with a wild glint in its eye, a little hair on its chest.

I enjoy the art: photographs by a friend; the watercolors by the woman from Paris in blue and brown shades. Her two characters walking on a tightrope look like Estragon and Vladamir. The West German artist's 'noone lived in a pretty how town, with up so many hills down,' miniature trees and houses in reds and beiges and greens.

As I leave the gallery through the etched glass door, I see her —the woman with the red lips—laughing. I see only her red lips, her aqualine nose. I see her in every cubist painting, in Calder's wire sculptures, in Lautrec's cabaret dancers. Her figure is matronly, but not fat, and her hair color doesn't matter—blonde, brown, black. When she laughs her small eyes close as if they weren't there. Her laughing red mouth, protruding lips open—she is the clown, the whore, the bourgeoisie woman, the adultress, the lover, Germany in 1929, Chaucer's Wife of Bath made respectable.

At home, the box from my grandfather's store in Topeka catches my eye: "Locks & Hardware" printed in large blue letters on its comfortable, unvarnished surface, a far place from the stained glass, wrought iron, white walls and stainless steel of the gallery, from the liver pâte, the cheese, the good wine served only in liter bottles. Solid and wood. Locks and hardware.

I HAVE NOTHING TO WRITE ABOUT

(and this is a love poem)

Let me write about the presidential hopeful who just announced his candidacy by saying: We will advance! We will fight! March! Battle! I cringe at his words. Freud said, in the beginning, words and magic were the same.

Let me write about snow. Yes, snow. That clear air, wet snowflakes on your tongue. Earth rests, protected by snow's warmth. We trace our way through white, see the small prints of other creatures, the yellow lines on the highways wear thin until summer renewal.

Let me write about the petite woman who lives across the hall. I hear her arguing vehemently in Russian with her brother, Abe, who lives at the other end of the hall. After her trip to San Francisco, she tells me Minneapolis is too quiet, too small. She is from Moscow. She likes the "big city", house backed against house, people everywhere. I see Leningrad Square in winter. And the ballet. Oh, the ballet! she says. And on this quiet street the neighborhood wants to convert to a two-way, because the traffic is too noisy, I hear the bells of the Greek Orthodox Church every day at noon and six; it is quiet as an English village.

Let me write about Venice, California, in *Picture* magazine, where they roller skate to disco in the streets. One picture of a Black man and woman, faces ecstatic, not looking at the camera. Crowd shots, and shots of men performing disco—skate feats, jumping over barrels, dancing. The inevitable women in bikinis—too passive through the male photographer's eyes.

Let me write about Lake Calhoun on a semi-grey day. Canadian geese feed in a green circle, half-covered with snow. A man squats at their center, pounding, cracking open something— food. Few ducks are left. A mallard feeds, his brown mate blends closely with the shore. Fly south!

Runners, still out in force, wear brightly colored sweat suits. They have worn a smooth place on the sheen of ice on the path. The lake, not yet frozen, reflects the grey sky—a winter lake, but not foreboding. The day is not cold; but the chill on the windward side blows through me.

RIDING THE 21A

(May 7, 1979)

She is beautiful, that Black woman on the porch of the old house, lime paint peeling. Child of four or five and husband. She is talking to him. Her hair in braids. Selby-Dale. The Inner City Youth Center with lots of Black faces hanging out and a block down the Black kid about fourteen who hangs in the doorway of a store, looking toward the Center, like he wants to be there, but thinks maybe it isn't "cool." The abandoned houses with no windows. The red brick Victorian hotel across from W.A. Frost's restaurant with the arches and Victorian windows, glass after glass broken in, old shades blowing in some windows near the top turrets. F.Scott Fitzgerald's hangout, the Commodore Hotel, two blocks down, is burned out now. This is the neighborhood where a year ago my car ran out of gas, and two Black men pushed it out of the street for me—a sweet favor.

"What's going down man," the Indian man in the back of the bus says to the child of the Black woman who sits next to him.

We are going over the Mississippi River at Lake Street, crossing from St. Paul to Minneapolis, and the bus goes slowly and roughly along this bridge with the old streetcar tracks. The banks of the river are the fresh green of spring, and the University's rowboat crew is out practicing—a motorboat alongside.

The fire engine at the Poodle Club on Lake Street—the Indian man tells the boy, "Look man, a fire engine." Adults will never stop pointing out fire engines to children.

A man scares me, almost landing in my lap from the jerk of the bus. He apologized laughingly in his Swedish-American accent.

An Indian woman and three children get on the bus, and another woman with a tomato plant, a small child, and a picture of Popeye's Olive Oyl on the back of her T-shirt, gets off the bus at Cedar Avenue.

The sign on the side of a building says:

The flag flies high from the tower of the original Sears-Roebuck Store, SEARS in large green letters on the grey concrete. I don't see downtown and the sleek glass of the IDS Tower from here.

the rooms above Mousey's Bar
a sunny fall afternoon

she leans out the window
body thrust forward
and spits
onto the sidewalk

she settles back in a blue nightgown
that matches her pale skin,
caught between the window frame
and a white sheet curtain

I want to be a photographer
a painter, anyone who can
capture her face
skewed at once in pain and sadness
she is not young, not old
she carries her years like
extreme unction

her lips all angles, out
of proportion, a cubist painting,
her hair brown, soft, looks like
she just washed, curled it
but has no fire, her face,
body, passive
disappointed, resigned

I want to rush to her and say
No. You don't have to stay here.
It's not even where
the classy hookers hang out

I am trapped in the bus
as it moves past the brick
and movie marquees of Hennepin Avenue

she'd probably say
"Who the hell are you?"

BUT THAT WAS IN ANOTHER COUNTRY

(for Sharon)

It is so easy to close the eyes
not to know the violence in the air;
the scream next door when it appears
to come from another country,
the cry from another country
when it could be next door.

The news comes quickly by phone.
He has gouged out one eye.
The other might be saved.
She cries for him. Why? Why?

Ax Murderer Kills Daughter:
but that was a generation ago,
before she knew him,
heroin and acid ago.
Now the eyes.

And I ask, too, why into my comfortable world?
This man is all my friends from the war years;
he is a generation of American men. This man,
who puts out his eyes.

This man did not massacre people in Vietnam.
He did not even fight. The wounds of those years
sting our veins and marrow,
hold, in our blood.
We do not know how many are lost —
they haunt us

This land did not suffer defoliation,
mine scars, bombs to violate the earth
instead of the plow and seeds to follow.
But the terror still
                    sears the mind's eye.

He is only one of many:
    "I went to prison rather than fight. I was
    the woman, taken in violence. My girlfriend
    would come to see me; we'd hold hands across

    a table in the visitors' room."

    "It was a peaceful sit-in. They came
    in the night, tried to give us clubs
    with spikes from the backs of vans."

    And the slit eye, the contorted figures,
    the horrific images of my artist friend.
    Out of what do they rise?

eyes
eyes to the soul
eyes we would all close
until he puts them out
to see

drugs to heal the body
drugs to make us forget
when the soul aches
the soul grieves

waaaa   haaa   laaa
where are those ancient words
we have no language for grief

I want to mourn for him
for all my brothers
for all my sisters

carry me to see
my body sways
waaaaa   haaaa   laaa

before rebirth
must come death and mourning
have we forgotten how to mourn
how to cry with the heart

Sing, my heart, sing
waaaaaa haaaaa laaaaa
   waaaaa   haaaa   laaaa
      waaaa   haaa   laaa

SUMMER SOLSTICE

(for a friend)

Slowly we cast the circle
naming east, south, west, north
here, by the river
wind filtering through birch trees
silvery leaves turned to the sun

the circle cannot be broken

Here, by this river
on sand and stone
sun in full view
Our ancestors knew better
than we who live in cities
sun and moon blocked
by rows of houses
and fear

Were by grandmothers
witches burned at Salem
No, more likely they were the burners
those who cried, Witch!
for fear their own hearts
would come home

Here, in this circle
I am strong
We burn away
the evils of ourselves
wrongs done to us
Here is no evil
only a cleansing
No god of guilt and sin
ever lifted me
on the wings of my own being
and said,
you are home

One by one the women speak
When my time comes
I can think of nothing
good about myself
Only months later,
alone, in sadness
I remember:
I am smart, I am strong
I am good
the circle
will not be broken

You are more fragile than a flower
like the wings of a maple seed
you soar on the wind
When I hold you
a rain of sweetness,
a drop of water on a white petal
after summer rain,
opens my heart, my body
trembling, translucent,
I sing for you

the circle will not be broken
the circle, the circle
winds in the wind
We dance, hands joined,
in a spiral through the sand
and I hear you
in the turning birch leaves
see you in the river
feel you in the sun, the sand
coursing through my bare toes

I touch the earth, the stones
as I do not touch you
except in my dreams
and I know
my strength, my fragility
full circle
and I am home

IN THE MEANTIME

in the meantime
    life gets more complicated
    the radio plays the piano
    the mirror waits anxiously to be hung

red Quixotes pass between the windmill slats
    catch me in small vortexes
    of transparent thread

The psychedelic poets are dead now
    they went out crying in bright colors
    about the demise of almost everything

instead there are fern fronds waiting to unfold
    elegant as ostrich plumes
    green and fecund

in the meantime
    rain falls
    sun shines
    on this small space

III

You wove our hair of darkness
our skull of dawn
our flesh of red-white stone

of stone   water   fire   blood
you make children grow inside women
plants come to life
earth sister, mother
yellow gold cosmic egg, seed of the world
Queen of Bright Night and Darkness
guide to lost travellers
pathway to visions and sleep
spirit of the underworld, ruler of madness
home of the dead awaiting rebirth
home of souls unborn
Queen of Darkness
You rise from death to fire

FEMALE CHILD POEM

(from the childhood victim of a rapist)

it is like that
love, sex, pain

they try to make you believe many things
they try to fool you
do not believe them
they tell you not all men are evil
and you ask them to prove it
they will not be able to

they will stick splinters in your
vagina, to torture you
they'll make you eat shit
that will only be the beginning
when your body is old enough
they'll start abusing it
then they'll break your heart

no man will ever love you because you are cursed
not with the blood that flows from your body
but with the curse
that men have imposed on you
they will call you girl
treat you like a child
they will tell you
you have no brain, only a body
are fit only to be their servant
they will rip your children from your womb
with their selfishness and leave you barren

when your body is old, they will shed you
like a snake skin and slide
into the next fresh young body they can find
you don't know the story of Eve? how the serpent tempted
her? the serpent was the evil side of god/man
but they put the blame on woman

they will only hurt you again and again
they will torture you with their games, betray you
rape you, desert you, sing sweet songs of love to you
only to rip your heart out and pulverize it
they will make you hate them, they will hurt you
until you have no choice
but to hate them

You, innocent child
wanting to believe
do not believe
do not believe them

IN TOTO

the box on the cabinet
is lacquered Chinese red

in that box are all
the documents of my life

    bank accounts
    life and health insurance plans
    unemployment records
    official transcripts
    birth certificate

it does not contain
the unwritten symphony

    to Blake's "Mental Traveller"
    that resounds note upon note
    in toto
    in the confines of my head

it does not contain
the silent side of me

    the red mouth
    that spins words at me
    ringed with fire
    I can outdo Prometheus
    I too am chained —
    by fetters of words
    that fall so easily
    from the red lips of others

I am mute
in the terrors
inside this red night
quiet in the disciplinc
of separating
chaff from grain
in the wag of tongues
thought spoken
the word become flesh

this red box does not contain

A WOMAN DYING OF CANCER

I watch late afternoon sunlight
spot the grey house across the street
I wonder how much longer
I'll be able to see

    the light
    the sun
    perhaps because I had two
    blind grandmothers
    light is so important to me
    I drown myself
    in light
    there are days
    even rainy days
    when light is my salvation

what you want from me
I cannot give you
I want to give you myself
that is all I can give you

if I die of cancer . . .
if there is a nuclear holocaust
what will we be
will we be at all

    if i die of cancer
    if I die
    will you all live on
    in peace

if I die
do not desert me
promise me
you will not
die too
of waste
of dreams of power
of power plays
and war

promise me
a vision of peace

    and yes, of love
    and keep your promise

CLIPPED WINGS

The lake is calm
clouds of pink lace
in blue water
yellows align the shore
reflections
captured on water-light

I run, breathless
through geese feeding and quacking—
tell them to fly south before snow falls
before they are trapped
at the end of the lake for winter
where open water is kept for those
with clipped wings

And I run harder, one foot after the other
beating on tar, making invisible tracks
indelible only to me
as I pace off the lake
a fall day
the red-gold glory
the clear irony of living

INTERMEZZO

this cool evening
I walk and walk in anger
in this downpour
wet to the skin

what is gone
the desire or the touch
red blossoms no longer
line the window sills of my dreams
in neat rows

now branches knit together, arch a road
flood with golden green light
as the sun plays havoc
to revel in earth's marrow
to remember on sleepless nights

a seed pushes slender, greenwhite
out of dark soil
a dew tear resting
on its small shepherd's crook
crowned with leaves

let her hair entwine you
wrap you about

the moon is your sister
your hair, your throne

the moon looms large and ripe
in the late summer sky

      gold on gold
      a wedding band

in early spring
the moon is small and milk-white

      her cresent your cradle
      the mother of awakening

TELEGRAM TO GOMORRAH

ring around the rosy
pocket full of posy
ashes
ashes
we all fall
down
down
ashes
to ashes
dust to dust
blessed
is one who
the rain falls on

ashes, ashes
we all turn to dust
roses and posies
to keep the rotten
smell away
that Black Death

this is the White Death
the mushroom death
white heat
shadows
mere shadow

if we do not

STOP

1984

1

how is it I lose my best self
to this slow methodical
death of television
of nights spent in restless staring
at a shadow box
until I too am shadow

here are no
similies, no metaphors
only the sense of separateness
the isolation of a lone wildflower
that blooms on the timber line
slips into oblivion without
eyes having said yes
reseeds itself before the ground
grows hard against entry
as this land has grown

every night lines form
at the churches for free dinners
at the shelters for a place to sleep
we watch
we wait
in Hong Kong they riot
in Rome, the Pope prays for peace

I see lines of bag ladies
in Newark Station
in Guatemala
women are killed
by being forced to allow worms
to lay eggs in fresh wounds
and guarded from help
until they die, day by day
in agony

2

I am mesmerized by the flick of the TV
its droning sound
lulled into complacency
like the victim
of a lizard sunning on a rock —
at any time its fast tongue
can flick out
to unsuspecting prey

who is the lizard
greedy and lean
who the wildflower
that asks, takes
so little from the world
for its brief stay

I know the women in Guatemala
are the wildflowers,
the patrones, the lizards
except they grow fat on their kill

and unlike the wildflowers,
the women who die of worms
labor with great tiredness
for the nothing they receive

I tell you nothing
you do not already know

day unfolds day
the world
like the wildflower
the lizard's tongue
and we watch
as we watched old war movies
and news clips of Vietnam
until we could not tell
the difference
between reality and fiction

the distinction was lost, because
both came, in living
color, from a box
of shadow

now an image can be
reproduced perfectly
and it is further from the truth
than the primitive drawings
of the cave people

3

It is not enough
we must move beyond shadow:

our *lives* are our images
made of light, not shadow
to shape them to peace
each individual's gesture
to ring in history

until one collective voice —
one image of the heart
made of many sounds
many gestures
many lives —
resounds
in peace

the texture of the air
after a nuclear explosion
jammed with infinitesimal
radioactive stutterings
after the flashes
after the blinding light
red-hot
orange-blue, pink and yellow
the teapots disintegrate
flesh disintegrates
the black mushroom
hangs in the air

today in Paris it is spring
the Seine flows
lovers walk across
traditional bridges

today in my back yard
the lilacs bloom
their fragrance subtly floods the air
each succulent tendril, each blossom

the survival of the fittest
lilacs are fittest
and the slugs that come
out from under the sash
of the back door each spring

is the human being fittest
centuries of war
blood and bones
blood and bones
blood and bones

now
the mushroom cloud
are we fit enough
to save ourselves

like the grey slug
the lilac bush

ALLEGRO RISOLUTO

Signs on the wind
imprint of crows' feet
the shadows of the days are longer

I do not recognize myself in the mirror
the small eyes, severe face

I am almost forty
yesterday I was twenty
the years have etched themselves on a pane of glass
translucent, I look as through a mirror:
I am young and slim, angry and sad

Always, I have turned to the wind
sought the grass the sky the water
these have been my resting places
alone, I have sought the solace of wind and rain
I do not fear the lightning

In my dreams I catch falling stars
I hold the moon in my palm
my heart has not changed
I learn to wear my new body with grace

THE BLOOD OF OUR MOTHERS

(for the women of the Minnesota Women's Peace Camp)

And you will hear us speak
some of us gay as the new moon
some straight as the wind
husbands, lovers, children
gathered around us

the power of women unleashed
is the power of civilization
not barefoot and pregnant
no, these women
again and again
raise the children
give their unyielding strength
these are women of legend
whose tales of courage
and terror far outweigh
those of heroes of battle
they suffer and struggle on
and suffer
and struggle on

we will speak
until we are heard
survival is the subject
we know best

there will be no
nuclear holocaust
the crazy people will not take
our children from us
we will not let them
destroy the fullness
the roundness of earth
the orange sands
the blue, grey and green of sky and water
the green and yellow
that grows everywhere
the animals and insects
the fish and coral

We will speak until we are heard
from the Thames to the Tiber
the Yellow River to the Ganges
the Nile to the Mississippi
the Seine to the Amazon
the Don to the Rhine

in us run the waters
of the earth
the blood of our mothers
a rainbow of light and water
we shall not be moved
until the birth tree's
wailing is finished
until the earth rejoices
her travail ended

and the moon dances around the earth
new moon to full
perfect in her changing

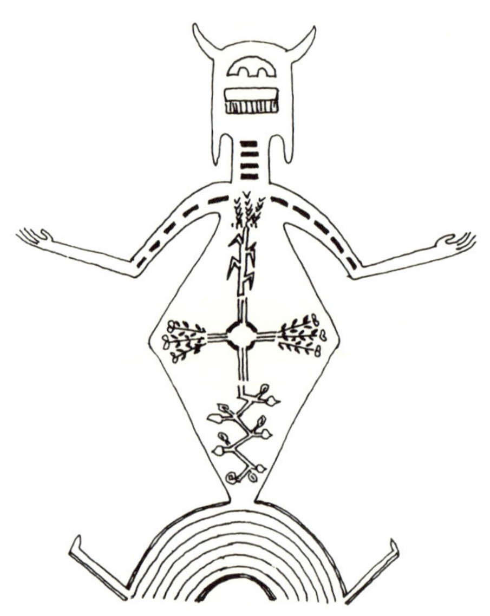

Thanks to the following people who helped make
this book possible: Polly Mann, William E. Bright,
Gloria Lane Cushing, Barbara B.Brown, Bettye Givens,
Mary Kay Rummel, Barbara Sperber, Marlene Vernon,
Mary Ellis Peterson, Nancy and Maynard Jones.

With special thanks to my teachers, Michael Dennis Browne, Jim Moore, John Minczeski, and Patricia Hampl, to the Ragdale Foundation of Illinois for the time to work on the manuscript, to the members of Onion Skin for their help and support, to Susu Jeffrey for her invaluable editing, and also to Karla Andersdatter for her editing help, and to Susan Bright of Plain View Press for making this book possible.